SCHIRMER'S LIBRARY
OF MUSICAL CLASSICS

Vol. 2062

SCOTT JOPLIN

Selected Piano Rags

Also available in
Schirmer's Library of Musical Classics:
Scott Joplin: Complete Rags, Vol. 2020

ISBN-13: 978-1-4234-1784-2

G. SCHIRMER, *Inc.*

DISTRIBUTED BY

HAL•LEONARD®
CORPORATION

7777 W. BLUEMOUND RD. P.O. BOX 13819 MILWAUKEE, WI 53213

SCOTT JOPLIN
(1868–1917)

Scott Joplin was born in Texarkana, probably on what is now the Arkansas side of the line, in 1868. His mother had been a freewoman since birth; his father, newly emancipated, had been a performing musician in his slave days.

In spite of poverty, the young Joplin had an early education in music and a reasonably serviceable upright piano for his eager practicing. Not much is known of Joplin's early years. He is said to have left home at 14 after a dispute with his father over his ambition for a career in music rather than a working trade. His wanderings as an itinerant pianist and entertainer in the 1880s and '90s took him throughout the Midwest, with long stops in Chicago and St. Louis. During these *wanderjahre* Joplin absorbed the rich layers of music in that Mississippi Valley heartland, and, equipped with formal training acquired where and when he could find it, plus a rare mixture of inborn talent, classical discipline and folk understanding, he developed his superb piano music. As Rudi Blesh wrote in his introduction to *The Collected Works of Scott Joplin*, Joplin "effected a basic and altogether remarkable fusion of Afro-American rhythm, American folk song both black and white, and the musical principles and procedures that America has traditionally derived from and shared with Europe."

In the late 1890s Joplin settled in Sedalia, Missouri—a tough rail-head town with a prosperous "district" and plenty of jobs for good players. He soon became the leader of the black musical community as well as a popular entertainer, and though still only in his late 20s, the sought-after mentor of younger player-composers. It was in Sedalia that the famous *Maple Leaf Rag* was first published by John Stark and Son, and where the outlines of other Joplin rags were first sketched.

The mirror image of Joplin's initials and those of his publisher John Stark has intrigued many who look for a mystical relationship between these two men of different races and divergent worlds, meeting in Sedalia in 1899 and making almost instant musical history with the publication of the *Maple Leaf Rag*. John Stark was not the first to publish ragtime; other rags were being published elsewhere, including Joplin's first, *Original Rags*, issued by Carl Hoffman in Kansas City. But Stark brought total dedication to his publishing enterprise. The Stark imprint was a proud one; it heralded the classics in ragtime's otherwise teeming mediocrity. The tough but sensitive John Stark, nearing what would be called retirement age today, came to the publishing business as a novice. But for 20 years, even until his death in 1927, he championed against all odds the publication of classic ragtime as art, as *music*, finally losing money but working away at it, printing the music exactly as his gifted composers penned it, loving the rags and promoting them with untiring zeal.

Backed by Stark, Joplin returned to St. Louis at World's Fair time, and in those first years of the new century that city teemed with action and ferment. Every ragtime player worth half his salt hit town for the good money and eager crowds, and St. Louis established a reputation that is still acknowledged—the home of classic ragtime. During these crucial years Scott Joplin channeled his pent-up creativity into the precise style of the piano pieces published here.

Joplin, restless again, left St. Louis in 1907, moving first to Chicago and then to New York, where his professional life quickened and his composing genius flowered anew. It was during these New York years that he devoted more and more time to his beloved project, the opera *Treemonisha*, a project doomed to failure, a failure that surely hastened his death. Scott Joplin died in New York City on April 1, 1917, the week that America entered World War I. Sweeping changes were in store for the nation.

Joplin's music lay dormant for many years, cherished by a few collectors and relished by pianists lucky enough to stumble upon dog-eared original copies in a piano bench or music cabinet. Joplin was very much of his time, recognized and respected by fellow musicians and known to a music-hungry public. If that public was unaware of the details of his life, if it did not follow his tortured career to its tragic finale in a charity hospital on Wards Island; if indeed it had forgotten or never known that this gifted artist was a black man trapped in prejudice and circumstance, it did know his music. *Maple Leaf Rag* may be the single most successful composition in the history of popular music—a piece that influenced every composer and pianist for many years, and which established the form and content of classic piano ragtime during its startling sweep of public acceptance at the turn of the century.

—Max Morath

CONTENTS

THE CASCADES
A Rag

Tempo di marcia

Fine

THE CHRYSANTHEMUM
An African-American Intermezzo

Introduction
Slow march tempo

1904

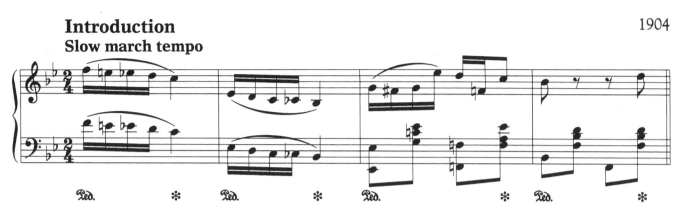

Fine

ORIGINAL RAGS

* Picked by Scott Joplin
1899
arranged by Charles N. Daniels

* "Pick," in 1899, was a slang term for playing ragtime piano; Daniels was a staff arranger at the original publisher, and undoubtedly had little or nothing to do with the composition of this piece.

Fine

THE EASY WINNERS
A Ragtime Two-step

Introduction
Not fast

1901

Fine

REFLECTION RAG
(Syncopated Musings)

1917

Slow march tempo

Fine

This page has been intentionally left blank.

ELITE SYNCOPATIONS

Introduction

Not fast

Fine

Dedicated to James Brown and his Mandolin Club

THE ENTERTAINER
A Ragtime Two-step

Introduction
Not fast

1902

repeat R.H. 8va higher

Fine

SOLACE
A Mexican Serenade

1909

Very slow march time

MAPLE LEAF RAG

Tempo di marcia

Trio

Fine

Respectfully dedicated to the Five Musical Spillers

PINE APPLE RAG

Notice! Don't play this piece fast. It
is never right to play "ragtime" fast.
—Author

1908

Slow march tempo ♩ = 100

Fine

ROSE LEAF RAG
A Ragtime Two-step

1907

Notice! Don't play this piece fast. It
is never right to play "ragtime" fast.
—Author

Slow march tempo

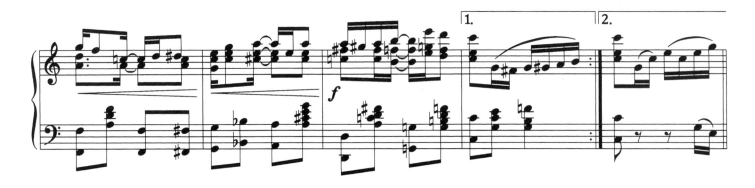

Fine

WALL STREET RAG

Notice! Don't play this piece fast.
It is never right to play "ragtime" fast.
—Author

1909

Very slow march time

Panic in Wall Street, brokers feeling melancholy.

Good times coming.

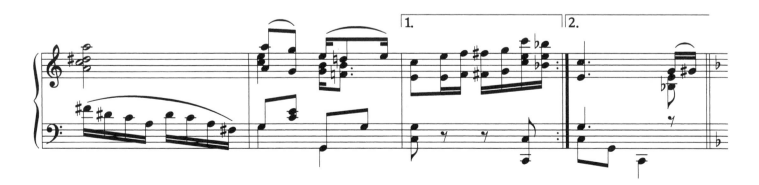

Good times have come.

Listening to the strains of genuine Negro ragtime, brokers forget their cares.

Fine

MAGNETIC RAG

1914

Allegretto ma non troppo

Tempo l'istesso

Fine